Fraud Aspect

Recognizing the Fraud Pattern: Hook. Story. Urgency. Action

Christopher Biggar

Dedication

For my family.

Copyright

 First edition. christopherbiggar.com

Acknowledgements

I want to thank the individuals who have supported me throughout my career and helped shape my perspective on fraud and financial crime. To the colleagues and mentors I've worked alongside, your experience, insight, and commitment to protecting others have played a meaningful role in how I approach this field. To my family, thank you for your continued support, encouragement, and understanding throughout this project. This work reflects not only my own experiences, but also the collective knowledge and dedication of those working every day to identify, prevent, and respond to fraud.

Disclaimer

The views and perspectives expressed in this book are my own and do not reflect those of my employer or any affiliated organization.

Contents

Introduction

It's not always complex schemes or highly technical attacks. More often, it's small gaps, overlooked details, and moments of trust that are manipulated at exactly the right time.

Working in fraud has changed how I see these situations. What appears obvious in hindsight is rarely obvious in the moment. Most cases don't happen because someone wasn't paying attention; they happen because the scenario felt legitimate.

Over time, I noticed patterns not just in the methods being used, but in how fraud unfolds. Regardless of the channel, whether it's a phone call, a check, a message, or an online interaction, the structure is often the same.

That realization became the foundation for this book.

Fraud Aspect is built on the idea that fraud is not random. It follows a pattern. Once you understand that pattern, it becomes easier to recognize, disrupt, and prevent.

This book is not meant to be overly technical or theoretical. Instead, it focuses on a real-world perspective: how fraud happens, why it works, and where systems and people are most vulnerable.

Fraud continues to evolve, but the underlying principles remain consistent. By understanding those principles, we can shift from reacting to fraud after it happens to recognizing it as it develops.

The goal of this book is simple: to provide clarity not just on what fraud is, but on how it works in practice, and how we can better respond to it moving forward.

Chapter 1

Fraud Has Changed, But Most Systems Haven't

It's easy to picture fraud as something highly technical or unusually complex. Those cases exist, but they are not what most institutions deal with day to day. Most fraud is quieter than that. It often grows out of small gaps, routine decisions, and behavior that looks ordinary on the surface. It does not usually break systems. More often, it works through them, and that is exactly what makes it dangerous.

Fraud has evolved faster than many of the systems built to detect it. Monitoring tools have improved, rules have become more refined, and institutions have become more aware of risk. But fraud has also shifted in ways those systems don't always account for.

Instead of becoming easier to spot, it has become better at blending into what already feels normal. It blends into expected activity and mirrors legitimate behavior. That creates the real challenge: fraud often looks acceptable until the damage is already underway.

The Evolution of Fraud

Most of the time, fraud relied on clear indicators: large, unusual transactions; unauthorized access attempts; activity that clearly deviates from normal behavior. Fraudsters understand thresholds, timing, and behavior patterns.

They know success doesn't always come from bypassing controls. In many cases, it comes from staying close enough to normal that no one reacts in time.

The System vs. the Environment

Fraud detection systems do not operate in isolation. They operate in an environment shaped by high transaction volume, time constraints, operational pressure, and human decision-making. Even when a system identifies a potential issue, someone still has to review it, interpret it, and decide what to do next. That process introduces risk, not because people are careless, but because the environment is complicated. Decisions are made under pressure, information is often incomplete, and priorities compete. Fraud does not have to defeat the system completely. It only must move through the surrounding environment.

The Shift Toward Behavioral Fraud

Modern fraud is not only a technical problem. In many cases, it is behavioral. Instead of attacking systems directly, many fraud scenarios now focus on influencing decisions before a transaction ever occurs. A customer may be convinced to move funds. In business, an employee may be instructed to change payment details. A user is prompted to provide credentials. In each case, the system may remain technically intact. The person interacting with it is the one being influenced. Once that happens, the system processes what looks like a legitimate action.

The transaction may be authorized, the login may be valid, and somebody may have approved the request. But manipulation shaped the decision, and that is where the real risk lies.

Why Detection Alone Is Not Enough

Most fraud strategies still lean heavily on detection: identifying suspicious activity, flagging unusual behavior, and blocking high-risk transactions. Those steps matter. But they are also reactive. They focus on the outcome, and by the time the outcome appears, the chance to prevent it has already narrowed.

That is because fraud usually begins well before the transaction itself. It begins with influence. It seems to stem from a message that appears legitimate: a phone call from someone trustworthy or known, or a request that seems genuine.

By the time the transaction happens, trust has often already been established, the story has already been accepted, and the decision has already been shaped.

A New Way to Think About Fraud

Understanding modern fraud requires a different way of thinking.

Instead of asking, "Does this look suspicious?" ask, "What made this look legitimate?"

That is where fraud gains its advantage, not in what is obviously wrong, but in what appears reasonable enough to move forward.

This shift changes the focus: from anomalies to patterns, from transactions to behavior, and finally from outcomes to progression. Once that shift happens, fraud becomes easier to recognize, not because it suddenly stands out, but because you start to see how carefully it fits in.

What This Means Going Forward

This is the foundation for everything that follows. Once you understand fraud as something that blends in rather than announces itself, it becomes clear that traditional approaches alone are not enough. Detection has to evolve. Processes have to adapt. And awareness has to move earlier in the sequence. Fraud is no longer just something happening outside the system. It often operates from within it, and recognizing that is the first step toward preventing it.

Chapter 2

The Gap Between Detection and Reality

Many people believe fraud detection systems are built to catch everything. If a transaction is suspicious enough, the assumption is that it will trigger an alert, be reviewed, and be stopped before any real damage occurs.

In theory, that sounds straightforward. In practice, it rarely works that cleanly.

Fraud detection is not only about identifying suspicious activity. It is also about managing volume, prioritizing risk, and making decisions under pressure. A system can generate alerts, but it cannot ensure someone interprets them, prioritizes them, or acts on them in time. That responsibility still falls on people, and people operate within constraints.

Time >Volume >Fatigue >Competing priorities

These four constraints create a gap between what detection systems can do and what happens in real-world environments. And that gap is where fraud often operates most effectively.

The Expectation of Detection

From the outside, fraud detection often appears straightforward. When a transaction occurs, if it appears suspicious, it is flagged. If it is flagged, it is reviewed. If it is confirmed as fraudulent, it is stopped.

This linear view creates an expectation that systems function with precision and consistency. Detection isn't a single step; it's a process involving multiple layers of evaluation, interpretation, and decision-making. Each layer introduces variability, and that variability creates opportunity.

The Reality of Volume

One of the biggest factors affecting fraud detection is volume. Financial institutions process thousands, and sometimes millions, of transactions every day.

Even with advanced tools, that activity can still produce a high number of alerts. Each alert points to a possible issue. Each issue needs review. And each review takes time. But time is limited, which means prioritization becomes unavoidable. Not every alert can receive the same level of attention. Some are escalated immediately. Others are delayed. Some are cleared quickly based on what is available in the moment. In some cases, alerts aren't reviewed within a meaningful timeframe at all.

This is not a system failure. But it creates a situation where fraud doesn't need to evade detection entirely. It only needs to avoid becoming a priority.

Decision Making Under Pressure

Fraud detection is not just a technical function. It is a human one. Analysts are required to interpret signals, assess risk, and make decisions, often quickly. Those decisions are not always clear. Information may be incomplete. Context may be missing. Signals may be subtle. At the same time, the cost of being wrong is high. Approving a fraudulent transaction results in loss; declining a legitimate one affects a customer. This creates tension, and under pressure, decisions often shift toward efficiency. Efficiencies such as faster reviews, quicker conclusions, and less time spent on borderline cases

Fraud does not need to be perfect. It only needs to exist within this environment. It only needs to be convincing enough to avoid deeper scrutiny.

The Fragmentation Problem

A message will introduce the situation. A call almost always reinforces it, then a transaction completes it. Somebody may review each step, and when viewed that way, it often appears legitimate. Often, there are no signs of fraud, and everything appears normal. The call sounds reasonable, and the transaction fits within the expected behavior.

The problem is that detection systems, and the processes around them, often don't connect with these events in real time. They evaluate pieces, not the full picture. And fraud operates inside that gap.

Timing as a Vulnerability

Timing plays a critical role in fraud detection. A delay often exists between when an event happens and when it is reviewed. A transaction may look normal in the moment. Only later, when supplementary context becomes available, does it begin to look suspicious. But by then, the outcome had already occurred.

Funds have moved. Access has been granted.

The opportunity to prevent it has passed. Fraud is strongest in real time. Detection is strongest in hindsight. And that difference creates risk.

A Real-World Example

The request is simple: update the payment instructions. Nothing about the request stands out. The relationship is real. The timing makes sense. The explanation is believable. The employee processes the payment. Days later, the real vendor follows up. **The payment was never received.**

From a detection standpoint, each step appeared legitimate. The email did not trigger concern. The transaction was within normal limits. There was no obvious anomaly.

The failure was not detected. It was in context. The full picture was never visible in time.

Reframing the Problem

Instead of asking: "Why didn't the system catch this?" A more effective question is: "What made this difficult to recognize in the moment?"

That's where the real challenge lies; fraud is not always hidden. More often, it is misunderstood. It appears normal because it is designed to appear normal. And when something appears normal, it is less likely to be questioned.

Closing the Gap

Closing the gap between detection and reality does not mean eliminating risk. It means understanding the conditions under which fraud succeeds. It means recognizing that detection is not only about systems. It is also about environment, Process, and behavior. It requires a different way of looking at the activity: from isolated alerts to connected activity, from individual transactions to sequences of events, finally from outcomes to the decisions that lead to them.

Because once those elements are understood, fraud becomes easier to identify earlier in the process, not after the fact, but while it is still unfolding. That's where prevention becomes possible.

Chapter 3

The Volume Problem

One of the most significant challenges in modern fraud detection is not complexity. It is volume. Fraud today does not need to outmatch the systems designed to detect it. It only needs to exist in an environment with limited attention and quick decisions. That environment is defined by volume. Transactions are constant. Accounts are accessed continuously.

Alerts are produced at scale, with each action creating data, and every piece of data can represent risk. But not all risks are equal, and that is where the problem begins.

The Scale of Modern Activity

Financial institutions process an enormous number of transactions every day. Payments, transfers, deposits, logins, and account updates all add to the activity being monitored. Detection systems evaluate that activity and identify potential issues, and they often do. But identifying a potential issue is only the first step. It still must be reviewed, interpreted, and acted on. That responsibility falls on people, and people have limits.

There is only so much time in a day, and only so much attention someone can apply, before fatigue sets in. As volume increases, those limits become harder to ignore.

The Burden of Alerts

Every alert represents a decision. It asks a simple question: is this legitimate, or is it fraud? That question is not always easy to answer. Alerts are not clearly fraudulent or clearly legitimate, but they do require judgment.

Judgment takes time, and in high-volume environments, time becomes the most
constrained resource. That forces trade-offs. Some alerts are reviewed quickly. Others are deprioritized. Some are resolved with limited information.

And in some cases, potentially important signals are missed entirely. This is not necessarily a system failure. It often results from an environment that makes thorough review difficult.

Prioritization and Its Consequences

When volume is high, prioritization becomes necessary. Not every alert can receive the same level of attention, so systems and the people using them have to decide what matters most. High-risk alerts move to the front. Lower-risk alerts are delayed or cleared. That approach is logical and necessary.

But it also creates an unintended consequence. Fraud doesn't always look high risk. In many cases, it looks average. It sits in the middle, not extreme enough to demand immediate attention and not safe enough to ignore entirely. In that middle space, it can be overlooked. Fraud does not need to avoid detection completely. It only needs to avoid prioritization.

Blending Into Normal Activity

The most effective fraud scenarios are designed with this in mind. They do not rely on extreme behavior or sharp spikes in activity. They stay within expected limits: a transaction amount in a normal range, a login from a familiar location, or a request that matches routine activity. Nothing looks unusual, so nothing is questioned immediately. Fraud hides this way, not by being invisible, but by being difficult to distinguish from legitimate activity.

The Role of Fatigue

Volume does not just affect systems. It affects people.

When analysts must review large numbers of alerts over extended periods, fatigue becomes a factor. Attention declines, patterns blur, and decisions are made faster with less scrutiny. This is not a failure of skill or effort. It is a natural response to sustained cognitive demand, and fraud exploits it.

Fraud doesn't need to be perfectly deceptive. It only needs to avoid triggering enough concern to warrant deeper review. In a fatigued environment, that threshold becomes easier to reach.

A Real-World Perspective

Consider a scenario where an analyst is reviewing alerts late in the day. They have already processed dozens, perhaps hundreds of cases. Most have been legitimate. A few have been fraudulent. The majority fall somewhere in between. Another alert appears. It shows a slightly unusual transaction, but not dramatically so. The amount is reasonable. The behavior is mostly consistent with past activity, and there is no clear indication of fraud.

Given the volume and context, the analyst clears the alert. Later, it is discovered that the transaction was part of a larger fraud event. From the outside, it may look like a missed opportunity. But within the reality of volume, it was a reasonable decision. And that is the problem.

Fraud often succeeds not because decisions are careless, but because they are reasonable given the information and constraints at the time.

Why Volume Changes Everything

Volume changes the nature of fraud detection. It shifts the challenge from identifying what is clearly wrong to recognizing what is subtly different. It reduces the time available for deep analysis. It also increases reliance on quick judgment.

It creates an environment where normality becomes a risk factor. When everything looks normal, it becomes harder to spot what isn't.

Rethinking the Approach

To address the volume problem, fraud detection must evolve. Focusing only on individual alerts or isolated transactions is not enough. The focus must shift to patterns, sequences, and behavior over time. Fraud is rarely a single event. It is a progression, and that progression often becomes visible only when you connect multiple events. That requires a different perspective, one that looks beyond volume and pays closer attention to how actions relate to one another.

The volume problem is not going away. If anything, it will keep growing. More transactions create more channels and more data.

The goal is not to eliminate volume. It is to operate effectively within it. That means recognizing that attention is limited, prioritization is necessary, and fraud will continue to exist in the spaces both create. Fraud does not need to overwhelm the system. It only needs to operate within it, and in high-volume environ environments, that is often enough.

Chapter 4

Fraud Doesn't Look the Way You Think It Does

Most people expect fraud to stand out. They imagine something unusual, something suspicious, something that immediately signals that something is wrong. But fraud rarely looks that way. In many cases, the most effective fraud does the opposite. **It blends in, mirrors legitimate behavior, and matches expectations.** As a result, people often accept it with little resistance. This is one of the most important shifts in modern fraud. It is no longer defined by what is obviously wrong, but by what appears completely normal.

The Misconception of Visibility

Many people believe fraud should be easy to recognize, that warning signs should be clear, and that something about the situation should immediately feel off. But fraud is not designed to feel off. It is designed to feel familiar. It may be a message that looks like it came from a known source or even a request that fits within an existing situation.

Nothing about it appears unusual. And that is exactly why it works. When something looks normal, people process it quickly, accept it easily, and rarely question it.

Familiarity as a Strategy

Fraud relies heavily on familiarity. It does not introduce entirely new scenarios. It mirrors existing ones. A customer receives a message about a transaction they recognize. An employee receives a request tied to a task they are already handling. A user is asked to verify information in a way that feels routine. Each of these situations exists in legitimate contexts. Fraud simply reproduces them. And when something feels familiar, it feels safe.

That sense of safety reduces resistance, lowers suspicion, and increases the likelihood that the interaction will continue. Fraud does not need to convince someone of something extraordinary. It only needs to reinforce what already seems possible.

The Role of Expectation

Expectations shape perception. People are conditioned to expect certain kinds of interactions. Banks do send alerts. Vendors do update payment instructions. Systems do require verification. These expectations come from real experiences. And fraud takes advantage of them. When an interaction matches expectations, it doesn't trigger concern. It fits within what is considered normal. Even if something is slightly different, it may not be enough to break that perception.

Because the overall structure still makes sense, fraud gains its advantage not by creating something new, but by fitting into what already exists.

When Normal Becomes Risk

The challenge is that normal behavior is no longer a reliable indicator of safety. A transaction that looks normal may not be legitimate. A request that feels routine may be influenced. A message that appears familiar may not be authentic. That creates a difficult reality: the very things that usually signal safety are now being used to create risk. Fraud does not stand outside normal activity. It exists within it. And that makes it harder to detect in real time.

The Importance of Context

To understand fraud, you need to look beyond the surface. A transaction, on its own, may appear legitimate. A login may seem valid. A request may feel reasonable. What matters is what led to it, the interaction, the timing, and the sequence of events.

Context provides meaning; without it, people can misinterpret actions. A transaction may be authorized. But why was it initiated? A login may be valid. But how was access obtained? Someone may fulfill a request, but what influenced the decision? These questions reveal fraud not in the action itself, but in the conditions surrounding it.

A Real-World Example

Consider a scenario in which a customer receives a message from their bank. The message indicates suspicious activity on their account. It provides a link to verify recent transactions. This is a common and expected type of communication. The customer clicks the link. After clicking the link, they are directed to a page that looks identical to their bank's website. They enter their credentials and confirm their information.

From the customer's perspective, everything makes sense. They expected the message, and once again the request was reasonable, and the process familiar.

But the interaction was fraudulent. Someone captured the credentials, granted access, and compromised the account. Nothing about the experience felt unusual because it was designed not to.

Why This Is So Effective

Fraud is effective not because it creates confusion, but because it creates clarity. In fact, it relies upon clarity, a clear explanation, and an obvious next step. When something is clear, it is easier to follow. And when it is easier to follow, it is more likely to be completed. That reduces hesitation, removes doubt, and increases the likelihood of action. Fraud does not overwhelm with complexity. It simplifies. And in doing so, it becomes more convincing.

Changing the Way Fraud Is Viewed

To address this challenge, we must change how we view fraud. Instead of asking, "Does this look suspicious?" the better question becomes, "Why does this look legitimate?" Because that is where fraud operates, not in what is clearly wrong, but in what appears completely right.

This shift moves the focus from surface-level indicators to deeper understanding. It encourages closer attention to context, greater awareness of influence, and earlier recognition of fraud, not because it stands out, but because it fits in too well.

The New Reality

Fraud is no longer defined by visibility. It is defined by invisibility within normal activity. It does not rely on breaking systems. It relies on working within them. It does not depend on obvious deception. It depends on believable scenarios. And it does not succeed because people are careless.

It succeeds because people are operating in environments where normal behavior is no longer a reliable indicator of safety. Critical understanding. Once fraud is
recognized as something that blends in rather than stands out, the approach to detecting it has to change. And that change begins with how it is perceived.

Chapter 5

The Illusion of the Obvious Threat

Many people believe fraud should be easy to recognize: if something is wrong, it will feel wrong, and clear warning signs will stop someone before they act. But fraud does not operate that way. It does not present itself as a threat. It presents itself as a situation, one that makes sense and feels familiar. That is where the illusion begins.

The Problem With Hindsight

After fraud occurs, everything becomes clear. The warning signs appear obvious. The mistakes seem avoidable. The outcome feels predictable. It is easy to look back and say:

- "Someone should have caught this."
- "This didn't make sense."
- "This should have raised concern."

But this clarity only exists after the fact. During the interaction, those same signals are rarely obvious. They are subtle, incomplete, and commonly overshadowed by urgency, context, and familiarity. What appears obvious in hindsight is rarely obvious in real time, and that gap is where fraud operates.

Reasonable Decisions in Uncertain Moments

Fraud does not rely on people making careless decisions. It relies on people making reasonable decisions based on incomplete information. The decision to act is not reckless. It is logical, given the information available at the time.

This is what makes fraud difficult to prevent. It does not exploit ignorance. It exploits context.

The Power of Partial Information

Fraud scenarios are often built on partial information. Enough detail to make the situation believable. But not enough to reveal the full picture. A customer may recognize a transaction. Maybe an employee recognizes a vendor, or a user may recognize a process. These pieces of information create confidence. They reinforce the idea that the situation is legitimate, but they do not tell the whole story. Without the full story, risk is harder to identify. Fraud does not need to provide complete information. It only needs to provide enough to move the interaction forward, justify the next step, and avoid deeper questioning.

Fraud often creates confidence through clear instructions, a defined process, and a specific outcome. This reduces hesitation. It removes uncertainty and encourages action. When a situation feels structured and controlled, it becomes easier to trust. Even if something feels slightly off, the overall clarity can outweigh that concern. Clarity creates comfort, and comfort reduces resistance. Fraud uses this intentionally by simplifying the interaction, removing complexity, and becoming more convincing.

The Role of Urgency in Masking Risk

Urgency plays a critical role in maintaining the illusion. It introduces pressure. It reduces time for reflection. It shifts focus from verification to action. Under normal conditions, a person may question a request. They may pause. They may seek additional information.

But urgency changes that. It creates a sense that immediate action is required. That delay may lead to negative consequences. That there is no time to verify. This does not eliminate doubt. It overrides it. The decision becomes less about certainty and more about timing. And when timing becomes the priority, scrutiny decreases.

A Real-World Scenario

Consider a situation where an employee receives a message from a senior executive. The message is explicit, references a current business matter, and requests a funds transfer. The mood is urgent, and the instructions are clear. From the employee's perspective, everything fits. The sender is known. The request is relevant. The immediacy feels justified. The action is taken. Later, they discovered the message was fraudulent. The executive never made the request.

The funds are gone. From the outside, it may seem like an obvious mistake. But at that moment, it was a reasonable decision. Everything made sense at the time. At that moment, the illusion holds.

Why the Illusion Works

The illusion of the obvious threat works because people don't perceive fraud as a threat during interaction. People see it as a situation that requires action.

No clear boundary exists between legitimate and fraudulent behavior. Context, familiarity, and importance shape perception. Fraud does not need to be perfect.

It only needs to be believable. And believability is often enough.

Breaking the Illusion

To understand fraud, you must break this illusion. Identifying what went wrong after the fact is not enough. You need to understand what made the situation seem right in the moment.

What elements created confidence? What signals were present but overlooked? What conditions influenced the decision? These questions lead to better prevention. Because once the illusion is understood, it becomes easier to recognize when it is forming, not after the fact, but during the interaction itself.

A Shift in Perspective

Instead of focusing on obvious threats, attention has to shift toward subtle influence.

"What feels right, but shouldn't?" This is a more difficult question, but it is also more effective. Fraud does not rely on being obviously wrong. It relies on being convincingly right.

The Reality of Modern Fraud

Modern fraud is not defined by deception alone. It is defined by perception. It succeeds when a situation feels legitimate, and it fails when that perception is challenged. That challenge does not come from systems alone. It comes from awareness, understanding, and recognizing that what appears obvious after the fact was not obvious in the moment. Prevention begins not by identifying clear threats, but by questioning what appears clear.

Chapter 6

Fraud Pattern

Fraud is not random, and it is rarely as unforeseeable as it first appears. At its core, it follows a structure: a sequence of events that moves from initial contact to outcome in a deliberate, repeatable way. That framework can be broken down into four stages:

Hook. Story. Urgency. Action.

These stages appear in nearly every fraud scenario, regardless of the method, channel, or target. They may take different forms or unfold at different speeds, but the pattern remains consistent. Once that pattern is understood, fraud becomes easier to recognize, not after the fact, but while it is happening.

Why Structure Matters

Most fraud detection focuses on outcomes. Outcomes from transactions, funds transfers, or logins. But these outcomes are only the final step in a much larger process. By the time the outcome occurs, the decision has already been influenced, the groundwork has already been established, and the person involved has already been guided toward a specific action. That is why focusing only on outcomes is limiting. It ignores everything that led to them, and that is where fraud develops. Understanding the structure shifts the focus once more:

- From isolated events to sequences
- From transactions to behavior
- From anticipation to reaction.

Fraud is not just something that happens. It is something that unfolds.

Stage One: The Hook

Every fraud scenario begins with attention, a moment where the interaction is introduced. This is the hook, and it can take many forms. It can show up as a message, phone call, an email, or even a notification.

The hook's purpose is simple. It captures attention, creates engagement, and initiates interaction. But it does not raise suspicion. In fact, the most effective hooks do the opposite.

They feel familiar. They feel expected. Nothing about the hook feels out of place. And that is intentional. Because once attention is captured, the interaction can move forward.

Stage Two: The Story

Once you've captured attention, the next step is to make the interaction make sense. This is where the story comes in. It provides context, explains why the interaction is happening, and answers a simple question:

"Why am I seeing this?"

A strong story is not complex. It is simple. It aligns with real-world experiences. Most times the hooks involve an account issue, delayed payment, or a verification request.

Each explanation is believable because it's familiar. They reflect situations people encounter regularly. The goal of the story is not to convince someone of something extraordinary. It reinforces something that already feels possible. When the story is accepted, the interaction becomes logical. And when something feels logical, people rarely question it.

Stage Three: Urgency

With attention captured and context established, the next step is movement. This is where urgency is introduced. Urgency creates pressure. It reduces time for reflection. It limits the opportunity to verify.

- **A deadline is implied.**
- **A consequence is suggested.**
- **A sense of immediacy is created.**

This shifts the decision-making process. Under normal conditions, people take time to evaluate. They consider alternatives and verify information. Urgency changes that. It moves the focus from "Is this correct?" to "What do I need to do right now?" That shift is critical.

Because when time is reduced, scrutiny decreases. Even if doubt exists, the need to act quickly often overrides it. This is where fraud gains momentum.

Stage Four: Action

The final stage is action. This is where the outcome occurs. And almost all the time, it involves a crucial moment: entering credentials or even providing private information. From the outside, this may look like the beginning of fraud. But it is the conclusion. The decision has already been made. The action completes the process. By the time this stage is reached:

Trust has been established between the customer and the fraudster. Their story was accepted, and the urgency reduced the customer's resistance. Everything feels justified. It feels like the logical next step. Because it feels logical, it gets carried out.

The Power of the Sequence

Each stage in the pattern builds on the previous one. The hook captures attention. The story creates understanding. Urgency drives movement. Action completes the outcome. Individually, each stage may appear harmless. But together, they form a structured progression.

And that progression is what makes fraud effective. It is not a single moment. It is a series of moments—each one designed to move the interaction forward.

A Real-World Example

Consider a scenario involving account takeover. A customer receives a message indicating suspicious activity. That is the hook. The message explains that their account may be compromised. That is the story. They are instructed to verify their information immediately to prevent further issues. That is urgency. They click a link, enter their credentials, and provide a verification code. That is the action. Each step feels reasonable, and every step makes sense. Together, they result in fraud. Not because any single step was obviously wrong, but because no one recognized the sequence as suspicious.

Why the Pattern Is Consistent

Fraud relies on behavior, and behavior does not change as quickly as technology. People respond to attention. They seek understanding. They react to urgency. They take action when something feels logical. These responses are predictable. And fraud is built around them. This is why the pattern remains consistent, even as methods evolve. The tools may change. The channels may shift. But the structure remains the same.

Using the Pattern to Prevent Fraud

Understanding fraud patterns creates an opportunity because it lets you identify fraud earlier in the process, before the final action occurs. Before the outcome is complete. Instead of focusing only on transactions, attention can shift to:

How did the interaction begin?

What context was provided?

Whether urgency is influencing the decision; this makes it possible to interrupt the process. To slow it down. To question it. And in doing so, prevent the outcome.

A Shift in Focus

Fraud detection has traditionally focused on results. But prevention requires a focus on progression, not just what happened, but how it happened. Once you recognize the pattern, fraud becomes less unpredictable. Not because every scenario looks the same, but because every scenario follows the same structure. That structure is what makes it understandable.

The Foundation for Everything That Follows

This pattern is not just a concept. It underpins understanding modern fraud. Every scenario that follows in this book will reflect it. Every example will reinforce it. Because no matter how fraud evolves, the underlying structure remains. And once that structure is clear, everything else becomes easier to see not just after the fact, but in the moment when it matters most.

Chapter 7

The Hook

Every fraud scenario begins with a single moment that, on its own, feels completely ordinary. A message appears, then a phone rings. An email arrives, then a notification is triggered. Nothing about that moment feels dangerous, and that is exactly why it works. This is the hook: the entry point into fraud. It is the first step in the sequence, and while it may seem small, it is one of the most important stages in the entire process. Without the hook, nothing else happens.

The Purpose of the Hook

The goal of the hook is not to deceive immediately, overwhelm, or create suspicion. Its purpose is simpler than that. It captures attention, creates engagement, and opens the door to interaction. If the hook fails, fraud stops before it begins. If it succeeds, the process moves forward.

Familiarity Over Suspicion

The most effective hooks do not feel suspicious. They feel expected. They align with situations people encounter every day. Text involving messages from banks, delivery notifications, and account activity. A request tied to an ongoing task. These are not unusual scenarios. They are part of normal life, and that is what makes them powerful. When something feels normal, it does not trigger hesitation. The mind processes it quickly, accepts it easily, and often acts on it without much thought. Fraud relies on this. It does not try to stand out. It tries to fit in.

The Timing of the Hook

Timing plays a critical role in how effective the hook becomes. A message received at the right moment feels more relevant. A call that aligns with a recent action feels more believable. A notification that follows expected behavior feels legitimate. Fraudsters understand this. They do not just send messages randomly. They position them after a transaction, during business hours, or at moments when a response is more likely. That increases the chance that the hook will succeed because relevance increases engagement, and engagement is the first step toward action.

The Simplicity of the Hook

The hook is rarely complex. In fact, the simpler it is, the more effective it tends to be. Messages are short, with clear statements and direct notifications.

No detail is needed at this stage. The goal is not to explain; it is to engage. Too much information can create doubt, and too much detail can raise questions. The hook avoids that. It provides just enough to capture attention and then moves the interaction forward.

A Real-World Example

I have even seen hooks that start with a customer receiving a text message from what appears to be their bank.

The message states: "Unusual activity detected on your account. Please verify immediately." This is the hook. It is short, direct, and familiar. It offers no detailed explanation or complexity. But it captures attention, creates concern, and prompts engagement. The customer clicks the link, and the interaction continues. At no point does the message feel unusual because it reflects something they have seen before. That familiarity is what makes it effective.

Why the Hook Works

The hook works because it does not ask for much. It does not require a major decision or demand immediate action. It simply introduces a situation.

Once you introduce that situation, the person becomes involved. Even a small level of engagement is enough.

- Reading a message.
- Answering a call.
- Clicking on a link.

Each of these actions moves the interaction forward. Once the interaction begins, it becomes easier to continue. This is how fraud builds momentum, not through large steps, but through small ones.

The Danger of Low Resistance

The hook is designed to have low resistance. It does not challenge the person receiving it. It does not create friction. It feels easy to engage with. That's where the risk lies.

Low resistance leads to quick responses; quick responses reduce scrutiny; and reduced scrutiny increases the likelihood of progression. The hook does not need to convince someone of anything. It only needs to get them to respond. Once that happens, the next stage begins.

Recognizing the Hook

Recognizing the hook is not always easy. Because it doesn't seem threatening, it looks routine. But there are subtle indicators.

- A message that creates immediate concern.
- A notification that prompts quick engagement.
- A communication that feels familiar but slightly unexpected. These are not definitive signs of fraud, but they are starting points. They are moments where attention should shift, not to panic, but to awareness.

The hook is not where fraud is completed. It is where it begins.

Why This Stage Matters

Understanding the hook changes how you approach fraud. It shifts the focus from reaction to recognition, and from outcome to origin. Instead of analyzing only what happened after the fact, you can focus on where the interaction started. If you can identify the hook early, you can interrupt the entire sequence.

- Before the story is accepted.
- Before urgency is introduced.
- Before action is taken.

A Shift in Awareness

The goal is not to avoid every message, call, or notification. That is not realistic. The goal is to recognize when an interaction is beginning.

- To pause.
- To consider.
- To ask: "Why am I being prompted to engage right now?" This small shift in awareness creates space, and that space allows better decisions. Fraud depends on movement. It depends on progression. When progression slows, the process weakens.

The First Step in Prevention

The hook is the first step in every fraud scenario, but it is also the first opportunity for prevention. If the interaction does not continue, the process stops. There is no story, no urgency, and no action- only a message that was not engaged with. That makes the hook more than an entry point. It becomes a moment of control, a point where the outcome can still be influenced before anything is lost, compromised, or moved forward.

Chapter 8

The Story

If the hook starts the interaction, the story keeps it moving. It answers the question that naturally follows any unexpected message, call, or notification: "Why is this happening?" Without that answer, the interaction feels incomplete, unclear, and easy to dismiss. With a believable explanation, it begins to make sense.

And once something makes sense, it becomes much harder to question. That is the role of the story. It turns attention into understanding and understanding into acceptance.

Why the Story Matters

The hook captures attention, but attention alone is not enough. A person may read a message, answer a call, or click a notification. Without a reason to continue, the interaction stops there. The story provides that reason.

- It gives context.
- It explains the situation.
- It creates a narrative that connects the initial contact to a logical outcome. Without the story, fraud feels incomplete. With it, fraud feels legitimate.

Believability Over Complexity

The most effective fraud stories are not complex. They are simple, clear, and grounded in real-world experiences such as an account issue, delayed payment, security concern, or even routine verification.

These are situations people encounter regularly. They do not require much explanation because they already make sense. Fraud does not introduce something unfamiliar. It mirrors something known, and that is what makes it believable. When something feels familiar, it is easier to accept.

The Structure of a Strong Story

A strong fraud story follows a simple structure. It identifies a situation, provides a reason, and points toward a solution. There are no unnecessary details and no complicated explanation, just enough information to create understanding. For example:

- "There has been unusual activity on your account."
- "Your payment details need to be updated."
- "We need to verify your information to avoid interruption."

Each of these statements introduces a situation and suggests action. They do not overwhelm. They are not confusing. They guide. That guidance keeps the interaction moving forward.

The Role of Context

Context is what gives the story power. Without context, a message is just a message. With context, it becomes meaningful and creates connections.

These connections create credibility. They reinforce the idea that the situation is real, even if the connection is only partial and only a small detail aligns. That is often enough, because the mind fills in the gaps; it assumes continuity and assumes legitimacy. And once that assumption is made, the story becomes stronger.

Filling in the Gaps

Fraud stories are rarely complete. They don't provide every detail or explain every element, and they don't need to. People naturally fill in missing information. If a message references a known vendor, the listener assumes the rest of the story. If a call mentions a recent transaction, the listener accepts the context. If a request aligns with an existing situation, it feels valid. Fraud relies on that.

It provides just enough information to trigger recognition, then lets the person complete the narrative. That makes the story more convincing, because it feels self-generated rather than imposed.

A Real-World Example

Consider a scenario involving a business email compromise. An employee receives an email that appears to be from a trusted vendor. The email references a recent invoice. It states that payment details have changed due to a banking update.

The explanation is simple, and the request is clear. From the employee's perspective, everything aligns. The vendor is known. The invoice is real. The situation makes sense. The payment is processed. Days later, the real vendor follows up. The payment was never received. Fraud is revealed. At no point did the story feel unreasonable, because it was built on real context, and that context made it believable.

Why People Don't Question the Story

People don't question the story because it doesn't give them a reason to. It fits within expectations, aligns with experience, and follows patterns they have seen before. Questioning requires friction. It requires uncertainty. It requires something that feels out of place. But a well-constructed story removes that friction. It provides clarity, creates direction, and reduces the need to question. This is not about carelessness. It is about perception. The story feels right, and when something feels right, people rarely challenge it.

Transition to Urgency

Once the story is accepted, the interaction reaches a critical point. The person understands what is happening, recognizes the situation, and sees the need for action. At this stage, there is still an opportunity to pause.

To verify. To question.

But that opportunity is about to change, because the next stage introduces urgency. And urgency shifts the decision-making process.

Why the Story Is So Effective

The story is effective because it does not try to deceive directly. It tries to make sense. It aligns with reality, reflects familiar situations, and allows the person to participate in the narrative. Fraud does not need to create belief. It only needs to support it. Once belief is established, the rest of the process becomes much easier.

A Shift in Awareness

To recognize fraud at this stage, attention must shift from the message's content to the context behind it. Instead of asking, "Does this make sense?" the better question becomes, "Why does this make sense right now?" That's where fraud operates: not in what is clearly wrong, but in what feels completely right.

The Second Opportunity for Prevention

The story represents a second opportunity to interrupt fraud, after the hook, but before urgency takes hold. This is the moment when someone can still question context and assumptions.

can still be challenged, and verification can still occur. But only if awareness is present. Once urgency is introduced, that opportunity shrinks, and the process accelerates.

The Foundation of Influence

The story is where influence takes hold. It shapes perception, guides understanding, and prepares the person for what comes next. Without the story, fraud has no direction. With it, fraud gains momentum. And once momentum begins, the outcome becomes much harder to change.

Understanding this stage is critical, because it is where fraud stops being an interaction and starts becoming a decision. That is what makes it so important.

Chapter 9

Urgency

If the hook begins the interaction and the story makes it believable, urgency is what drives it forward. It is the turning point, the moment when understanding starts to become action. Without urgency, most fraud would stall. People would pause. In fact, they would do what I always suggest. Pause, Verify, and Protect. They would take the time to think. But urgency removes that time. And when time is removed, decisions change.

Why Urgency Matters

Under normal conditions, people make decisions carefully. They evaluate information, consider alternatives, and verify what they are being told. That process creates protection. It introduces friction and slows things down, and fraud depends on removing that friction. Urgency makes that possible. It accelerates decisions, limits the opportunity for doubt to develop, and keeps the interaction moving.

The Shift in Decision Making

Urgency changes how people think. It shifts the focus from "Is this correct?" to "What do I need to do right now?" That shift is subtle, but powerful because it redirects attention. Instead of evaluating the situation, the person begins focusing on resolving it.

Instead of questioning the request, they begin to act on it. The goal is no longer to understand. It is to respond. And once that shift occurs, the likelihood of fraud increases significantly.

How Urgency Is Introduced

Urgency does not always appear as pressure. Often, it appears as necessity.

- A problem that needs resolving.
- A deadline that somebody must meet.
- A consequence that somebody can avoid.

The language is often simple:

- "Immediate action required."
- "This needs to be completed today."
- "Failure to respond may result in…"

These statements create a sense of importance. They elevate the situation and make it feel time-sensitive. When something feels time-sensitive, it becomes harder to ignore.

The Role of Consequences

Consequences often reinforce urgency. What happens if no action is taken? An account may be restricted, someone's payment may get delayed, or a service may be interrupted.

These consequences do not need to be extreme. They only need to be believable. The goal is not to create fear, but to create enough motivation to act before hesitation sets in. In many cases, avoiding a negative outcome feels more important than verifying the situation.

A Real-World Example

Consider a customer receiving a message that appears to be from their bank. The message states: "Your account has been flagged for suspicious activity. Immediate verification is required to prevent restriction."

The hook captures attention. The story explains the situation. And urgency introduces pressure. From the customer's perspective, the situation is clear: a potential problem, a need to act, and a limited window to do so. The customer clicks the link and enters their information. They complete the process. Fraud is complete. At no point does the customer feel reckless. They feel responsive, responsible, and like they are doing what is necessary. That is what Urgency is designed to do.

Why Urgency Overrides Doubt

Even when something feels slightly off, urgency can override that feeling. A small hesitation or moment of uncertainty may still be there, but urgency competes with it, and often it wins. Acting quickly begins to feel more important than being certain. The risk of delay

feels greater than the risk of error. At that point, the decision is made, not because doubt disappears, but because it is pushed aside.

The Compression of Time

Urgency compresses time. It reduces the window for decision-making, removes room for reflection, and limits the ability to seek additional information. That

compression matters because fraud does not benefit from extended analysis. It benefits from immediate action.

The shorter the time frame, the fewer questions are asked. The fewer questions asked, the smoother the progression becomes.

Urgency in Different Forms

Urgency does not always look the same. It can be direct: a clear deadline, a specific timeframe, or it can be indirect.

- A tone that suggests importance.
- A situation that feels time-sensitive.

- A request that implies priority. In both cases, the effect is the same. It creates pressure. It encourages movement. It reduces hesitation.

The Link Between Urgency and Action

Urgency bridges understanding and action. Without it, the process slows down. With it, the process accelerates. It turns a believable situation into a required response, moves the interaction from passive to active, and makes the final step much easier to reach.

Recognizing Urgency

Recognizing urgency is not about avoiding every time-sensitive situation. Many legitimate interactions require quick action. The difference lies in awareness: understanding when urgency is influencing a decision, not just what is being requested, but how it is being presented.

Instead of asking: "What needs to be done?" A more effective question becomes: "Why does this need to be done right now?" That question creates space. It slows the process. And slowing the process reduces risk.

The Third Opportunity for Prevention

Urgency represents the last meaningful opportunity to interrupt fraud before action occurs. After this stage, decisions are already in motion, and the focus shifts from evaluation to execution. But within urgency, there is still a brief window where awareness can change the outcome, a moment where someone can pause, take a breath, and verification can still happen. Even a small delay can disrupt the process, because fraud depends on speed. When speed is reduced, the process weakens.

Why This Stage Is Critical

Urgency is not just a step in the process. It is the catalyst. It turns belief into action, understanding into movement, and doubt into compliance. Without urgency, fraud struggles to progress. With it, fraud accelerates. Understanding this stage matters because it explains why people act even when something does not feel entirely right- not because they are careless, but because they are responding to pressure, and that pressure is intentional.

Once urgency has taken hold, the interaction moves to its final stage: action. By then, the outcome is already unfolding. The decision is made, the path is set, and the system is about to process what looks like a legitimate request. Understanding urgency makes that transition visible. It reveals the moment when everything changes. And once that moment is recognized, it becomes possible to respond differently, not after the fact, but in time to prevent the outcome.

Chapter 10
Action

If the hook begins the interaction, the story makes it believable, and urgency drives it forward, action is where everything is completed. This is the final stage, the point where the outcome becomes real. Fraudulent transfers are made, credentials are stolen or entered, and information is provided. From the outside, this is often where fraud is identified: the transaction, the login, the movement of funds. But this is not where fraud begins. It is where fraud ends, because by the time action occurs, the decision has already been made.

The Illusion of the Final Step

It is easy to focus on the action and see it as the moment when everything went wrong, the point where someone could have stopped the fraud. But that perspective is incomplete. Action is not the cause. It is the result. It results from everything that came before it. The hook captured the attention. The story helped someone understand the hook and believe it was real. The urgency drove someone to make a very decisive decision and then follow it with the action of losing funds.

Why Action Feels Justified

One of the most important aspects of this stage is that the action doesn't feel risky; it feels justified, logical, and even necessary. The person taking the action believes they are responding correctly. They believe they are solving a problem and following a legitimate process. From their perspective, that belief is reasonable, because every step leading up to the action supported it.

There is no sudden shift and no obvious moment of doubt, only a continuation of the interaction. This is what makes the final step so effective. It does not feel like a mistake. It feels like the right thing to do.

The Role of Trust

By the time action occurs, trust has already been established, not necessarily trust in a person, but trust in the situation. The message felt familiar. The explanation made sense. The urgency felt appropriate. Each of these elements contributes to confidence, and that confidence carries into the final step. The action is not questioned. It is executed because the situation, as it is understood, supports it.

A Real-World Example

Consider a scenario involving account takeover. A customer receives a message indicating suspicious activity on their account. They are prompted to verify their information. The message looks legitimate. The request makes sense. The urgency feels appropriate. They click the link.

They enter their credentials. They provide a verification code. From their perspective, they are protecting their account. They are responding correctly. But they have just provided access to a fraudster. The action was not reckless. It was reasonable, based on the information they had. That's what makes it so difficult to prevent at this stage.

Why Detection Happens Here

Many fraud detection systems focus heavily on this stage.

The transaction. The login. The movement of funds.

Because this is where the impact becomes visible, measurable, and flaggable for review, but by the time detection occurs here, the opportunity to prevent it has already narrowed. The process has already progressed. The decision has already been influenced. And the action has already been taken. This is why detection at this stage is often reactive. It identifies what has happened, but it does not always prevent it.

The Speed of Completion

Action often happens quickly. Once urgency has taken hold, there is little delay. The process moves from understanding to execution with minimal interruption. This speed is intentional. Fraud depends on it. Because speed reduces the likelihood of interference. The faster the action occurs, the less time there is for verification, consultation, or reconsideration. And without those interruptions, the process completes smoothly.

The Point of No Return

Action represents a critical threshold. Once it occurs, the situation changes. Funds are transferred. Access is granted. Information is exposed. At that point, the focus shifts from prevention to response.

- Recovery.
- Investigation.
- Mitigation.

These are important steps. But they are not the same as prevention. Because prevention requires intervention before this stage is reached.

Interrupting the Process

To reduce fraud, the focus cannot be solely on action. It must include everything that leads to it. By the time action occurs, the process is already complete in principle. The decision has been made. The outcome has been set. Interruption must happen earlier. It must happen during the first three stages: the hook, story, or urgency. These are the stages where influence is still forming. Decisions are still flexible, and outcomes can still change.

Recognizing Action in Context

When evaluating fraud, it is important to look beyond the action itself- not just what happened, but how it happened.

- What led to the decision?
- What influenced the behavior?
- What sequence of events created the outcome?

These questions provide insight, and they reveal patterns. Someone can use those patterns to prevent future incidents because isolated actions do not define fraud. Sequences define it. And understanding those sequences is key.

A Shift in Perspective

Instead of viewing action as the point of failure, it should be understood as the point of completion, the final step in a structured process. This shift changes how we approach fraud. It moves the focus upstream, toward earlier stages, influence, and behavior. That is where prevention is most effective.

The Completion of the Pattern

With action, the fraud pattern is complete.

Each stage has played its role. The hook captured attention. The story created understanding. Urgency reduced resistance. And action completed the outcome. But understanding this pattern does more than explain how fraud happens. It reveals how it can be stopped, not at the end, but at the beginning. That is where the real opportunity lies.

Looking Ahead

Now that the full pattern is clear, the focus can shift from how fraud happens to where it happens most often, from structure to application. The next chapters move beyond theory and into real-world scenarios where these patterns appear every day. And where understanding them makes the difference between detection and prevention.

Chapter 11

The Rise of Check Fraud and Social Engineering

Check fraud is often viewed as outdated, something tied to an earlier financial system and replaced by more modern schemes. But that perception is misleading. Check fraud has not disappeared. It has adapted. More importantly, it has merged with one of the most effective tools in modern fraud: social engineering. Social engineering is a form of fraud that remains relevant and, in many cases, increasingly effective.

Traditionally, check fraud involves direct manipulation: forged signatures, altered amounts, and stolen checks.

These methods depended on physical access and manual alteration. They were often easier to detect because the indicators were visible: inconsistencies, irregularities, and signs of tampering.

Modern check fraud looks different. The check itself is no longer the primary point of deception. It is the final step, the mechanism that completes a broader process. And that process begins long before the check is ever deposited.

The Role of Social Engineering

Social engineering changes the nature of fraud. Instead of targeting the check first, it targets the person. It shapes the situation, influences the decision, and builds trust before the check ever enters the process.

A customer is told they are about to receive funds. A believable explanation is provided. The check arrives, is deposited, and the money appears available. Then comes the next instruction: send a portion back, transfer funds, or make a payment.

At that point, the check is only part of the sequence. The real fraud happened earlier, in the interaction, the influence, and the decision that made the check appear legitimate.

A Common Scenario

Consider a scenario that appears simple on the surface. A customer is contacted with an opportunity and told they will receive payment. It may be for a job, a service, or sometimes a reimbursement. The explanation varies, but the structure remains the same. The check arrives and often looks legitimate. The amount is usually higher than expected, and an explanation is ready. The extra funds need to be returned or used for a stated purpose. The customer deposits the check. Funds appear available. They follow the instructions. They send money. Days later, the check is returned. **The loss is now real.**

Why This Works

This type of fraud works because it does not rely on deception alone. It relies on sequence. It relies on sequence.

- The hook introduces the opportunity.
- The story explains it.
- Urgency encourages action.

The check then completes the sequence. Each step feels logical, so the risk isn't recognized right away. The customer is not trying to bypass the system. They believe they are following instructions, and from their perspective, they are.

The Illusion of Available Funds

One of the most misunderstood parts of check fraud is fund availability. When a check is deposited, money may appear in the account before the check has fully cleared. From the customer's perspective, that looks like confirmation. The funds are there. Someone can use them.

That creates confidence and reinforces the belief that the check is legitimate. But availability is not the same as final settlement. That distinction matters, because fraud relies on the gap between deposit and return, the period when the funds appear real but are not.

The Timing of Fraud

Timing is critical in these scenarios. The request to send funds usually comes quickly, before the check has time to be returned and before anyone identifies an issue. This aligns with the urgency stage of a fraud pattern. It reduces the chance of delay, limits verification, and increases the odds that the action happens before the truth is revealed.

By the time the check is returned, the funds have already been moved. And recovery becomes difficult.

The Customer Perspective

From the customer's point of view, the situation feels legitimate. They received a check, deposited it, saw the funds appear, and followed the next instructions. At no point do they feel like they are committing fraud. They feel like they are participating in a transaction.

That is what makes social engineering so powerful. It does not force action. It guides it. And when action feels guided rather than forced, it is more likely to be completed.

The System Perspective

From a system standpoint, the activity may appear normal. A check deposit, a transfer, a withdrawal. Each action alone may not raise concern. There may be no obvious anomaly or immediate indicator of fraud. The system sees transactions. It does not see influence. That is where the gap exists.

Connecting the Pattern

When viewed through fraud patterns, the structure becomes clear.

- **Hook: An opportunity or payment is introduced.**
- **Story: A believable explanation is provided.**
- **Urgency: Instructions are given quickly.**
- **Action: Funds are sent.**

Each stage builds on the previous one. Each step moves the interaction forward. And by the time the final step occurs, the outcome is already in motion.

Why This Type of Fraud Is Increasing

This combination of check fraud and social engineering is increasing for a reason. It works because it leverages both systems and behavior. It uses traditional financial instruments. But it applies modern influence techniques to a traditional financial instrument. It does not rely on breaking controls. It relies on moving through them, and that makes it difficult to stop with traditional methods alone.

Prevention Through Understanding

Preventing this type of fraud requires more than monitoring transactions. It requires understanding the sequence, recognizing the interaction before the check is deposited, and

identifying the influence before the funds are moved. Because once the final step occurs,
the options narrow. Before that point, there is still an opportunity to question, verify, and slow the process, and slowing the process is often enough to disrupt the pattern.

Looking Ahead

Check fraud is not going away. It is adapting, evolving, and becoming more closely integrated with other forms of fraud. Understanding that evolution matters because it shows that fraud is not defined by the tool being used, but by how that tool is used. That idea carries into the chapters that follow, where different forms of fraud continue to reflect the same structure: different methods, same pattern, and the same opportunity to recognize it before it is complete.

Chapter 12

Account Takeover

Fraud does not always break into systems. Sometimes, it simply logs in. That is the reality of account takeover, one of the most common and most misunderstood forms of modern fraud. From the outside, it may look like a security failure, an unauthorized access event, or a credential breach. But in many cases, the system itself is not broken. The login is valid. The credentials are correct. The authentication process is completed. Yet the activity that follows is fraudulent because the real issue is not access. It is how someone obtained access in the first place.

The Shift in Account Access

Traditionally, unauthorized access required technical exploitation: Weak passwords, system vulnerabilities, brute-force attempts. These methods still exist, but they are no longer the primary approach. Modern account takeover often begins with influence rather than intrusion. A person is guided into providing access instead of having it forcibly taken. That changes the nature of the risk, because the system sees a legitimate user while the decision behind the action has been manipulated.

How Account Takeover Begins

Account takeover begins in multiple variations. The pattern is often the same. They can start with a message, a call, a notification, or something that requires attention. (This is the hook.) They can even come through as a security alert, a message about suspicious activity- you know, the one that we all seem to get? They often arrive as a request to verify account information. From the user's perspective, the interaction feels legitimate because it reflects something they have experienced before.

Building the Story

Once you capture attention, the next step is context. The story explains why the interaction is happening. It provides a reason and creates understanding.

- "There has been unusual activity on your account."
- "We need to verify your information."
- "Someone will restrict your access if you do not respond."

These explanations are simple but effective because they align with real-world experiences. They feel familiar, and when something feels familiar, it feels safe.

Introducing Urgency

With attention and context established, the agent introduces urgency. This is where the interaction accelerates.

The user is told to act quickly to prevent an issue or avoid a consequence. This reduces hesitation, limits the opportunity to question, and shifts the focus from verification to action. The user is no longer evaluating the situation. They are responding to it.

The Moment of Action

The final step is where access is granted. The user enters their credentials, provides a verification code, and confirms their identity. From their perspective, they are securing their account. In reality, they are granting access. The login that follows appears legitimate because it is. The system recognizes the credentials, and the authentication is valid. Without an immediate indication of fraud, account takeover is hard to detect.

Why It Looks Normal

From a system perspective, account takeover often appears as normal activity. From an inside perspective, it looks like a successful login, a recognized device, and a valid authentication process. There may be no immediate anomaly and no obvious deviation from expected behavior. The system sees access. It does not see influence. It doesn't know how someone obtained the credentials. It only knows that they are correct. And that creates a critical gap.

Activity After Access

Once access is obtained, fraud continues. Someone may update your information. Someone may add a new payee. Someone may transfer funds. Each of these actions may appear legitimate because they occur within an authenticated session. The system sees a user interacting with their account. It does not see the underlying reality that the user is no longer in control.

A Real-World Scenario

Consider a customer receiving a text message from their bank. The message states that there has been suspicious activity on their account. It includes a link to verify recent transactions. The customer clicks the link. They are taken to a page that looks identical to their bank's website. They enter their username and password. They receive a verification code, and they enter it as well. From their perspective, they have just secured their account.

Moments later, the fraudster logs in using the same credentials. They now have full access. They initiate a transfer. They move funds. The account has been taken over not because the system failed, but because someone tricked someone.

Why This Type of Fraud Is So Effective

Account takeover is effective because it leverages trust. It leverages trust in systems, communication, and in process.

The interaction feels legitimate. The request makes sense. The action feels necessary. There is no obvious deception, only a sequence of events that leads to access. And once access is granted, the rest becomes much easier.

The Limitations of Detection

Detecting account takeover is challenging because the signals are subtle. A login may occur from a new location, but that is not uncommon. A device may be unfamiliar, but that happens. A transaction may follow, but it may still fall within normal limits.

Each signal, on its own, may not be enough to trigger concern. When evaluated independently, those signals may never reveal a pattern. This is where detection struggles: not because the signals are missing, but because they aren't connected in time.

Prevention Through Awareness

Preventing account takeover requires shifting focus from access to what influenced it. Understanding how the interaction began can be a major part of preventing future account takeovers. Recognizing the sequence that led to the login is another major step. The key is identifying the signs of manipulation before credentials are provided, because once access is granted, the situation changes. The system sees legitimacy, and the window to prevent fraud narrows.

Connecting Back to the Pattern

Account takeover follows the same structure as every other fraud scenario. **Hook: a message introduces the interaction. Story: a situation is explained. Urgency:**

action is required quickly. Action: Credentials are provided.

Each stage builds on the previous one. Each step moves the interaction forward. And by the time access is granted, the outcome is already in motion.

A New Perspective on Access

A fraudster's access and patterns are based on behavior. Behavior is influenced and guided, which changes how we must address it. Securing systems is not enough. If the person using the system is influenced, the system will follow. Understanding that structure makes earlier recognition possible, not just when access is taken, but before it is given. That is where prevention becomes possible.

Chapter 13

Business Email Compromise

Fraud does not always target systems. Sometimes, it targets relationships. Business Email Compromise (BEC) is one of the clearest and most damaging examples of that shift: no malware, no obvious breaches, and no system failures. What you do have are messages, familiar senders, and a routine request. One small change can lead to a significant loss.

What Makes BEC Different

Unlike many other forms of fraud, BEC does not rely on breaking into systems. It relies on breaking into trust. The communication appears legitimate. The request feels familiar. The interaction aligns with real business activity. And because of that, it is rarely questioned in the moment. BEC does not introduce something new. It modifies something that already exists. It modifies the payment process, the invoices that go back and forth, the vendor relationship, and a routine task. That makes BEC extremely effective. It does not disrupt normal operations. It works within them.

How BEC Begins

Like all fraud, BEC follows a structure. It begins with the hook. An email arrives and appears to come from a known source.

- A vendor.
- A colleague.
- A senior executive.

The message is simple, often brief, and it references something familiar. Nothing about it feels unusual because it reflects real communication.

Building the Story

The next step is the story. The email provides context. It states a reason for the request or a change in process. It explains that an update is needed.

- "Our banking details have changed."
- "Please use this account for future payments."
- "There was an issue with our previous account."

These explanations are not complex. They are believable. They align with real-world situations, and that is what makes them effective. The recipient does not feel the need to question something that makes sense.

The Role of Urgency

Once the story is accepted, the sender introduces urgency. The payment needs to be processed. The most popular are. A deadline is approaching, or A delay may cause issues. This creates pressure. It reduces hesitation and shifts the focus from verification to completion. The recipient is no longer evaluating the request. They are executing it. That shift is critical because once urgency takes hold, the opportunity to question becomes much smaller.

The Final Action

The final step is the payment. Once this step is reached. The Funds are sent, and recovering the losses is hard. From the system's perspective, everything appears normal. The payment is authorized. The amount is expected. The recipient account is new, but not necessarily suspicious. The system may see no immediate red flags because it only sees a transaction. It doesn't see the conversation that led to it, and that is where the real risk lies.

A Real-World Scenario

Consider a company that regularly pays a vendor where invoices are received, and payments are processed. The relationship is established. An email arrives from the vendor. It refers to a current invoice. It says the payment details have changed because of a banking update. The request is simple. Update the account information and use the new details to make the payment.

- The explanation makes sense.
- The relationship is real.
- The process is routine.
- The payment is sent.

Days later, the real vendor follows up. The invoice is still outstanding. Somebody sent the funds to a fraudulent account.

Why This Works

BEC works because it aligns with normal business behavior. Employees are expected to process payments, follow instructions, and maintain relationships. The request does not feel unusual. It feels like part of the job, and because it does, people often complete it without hesitation. This is not a failure of awareness. It reflects how business operates. Processes are built for efficiency, speed, and completion, and BEC exploits that.

The Challenge of Detection

Detecting BEC is difficult because the signals are not always technical. They are contextual: A slight change in the email address. It may be a subtle difference in tone. Sometimes it involves a new account number.

Each of these signals may be small and easy to overlook, especially in high-volume environments where emails are processed quickly, requests are handled routinely, and attention is divided. Fraud does not stand out. It blends in, and that is what makes it dangerous.

The Role of Trust

Trust is central to BEC, not only trust in people, but trust in process. Employees trust that emails are legitimate, requests are valid, and systems are functioning correctly. BEC does not need to create that trust. It uses the trust that already exists. Once it leverages that trust, the process moves forward naturally.

Connecting the Pattern

Through the lens of fraud patterns, BEC becomes clear.

- Hook: An email introduces the request.
- Story: A believable explanation is provided.
- Urgency: The payment needs to be completed.
- Action: Funds are sent.

Each stage builds on the previous one. Each step feels logical. And by the time the final step occurs, the outcome is already in motion.

Prevention Through Process

BEC challenges a key assumption that fraud will be obvious and that something will feel wrong. But in BEC, everything feels right. Communication is familiar. The request is expected. The action is routine. And that is why it succeeds.

Looking Ahead

Business Email Compromise is not an isolated threat. It is part of a broader pattern, one that appears across multiple types of fraud, through different methods and channels, but with the same underlying structure.

Understanding that structure allows you to recognize it earlier. Not just when the payment is sent, but when you first receive the request. That's where prevention becomes possible.

Chapter 14

Where Fraud Detection Breaks Down

Fraud does not succeed because it is invisible. It succeeds because it is missed. That distinction matters because it shifts the focus from what fraud is doing to how it's understood. Most fraud detection systems are designed to identify anomalies such as unusual behavior, out-of-pattern activity, and clear deviations from what is considered normal. And in many cases, they do exactly that. They identify what stands out. But modern fraud is not designed to stand out. It is designed to fit in. And when fraud fits in, detection becomes much more difficult.

The Illusion of Coverage

A common assumption is that detection systems see everything. If something is suspicious, it will be flagged. If it is flagged, it will be reviewed. And if it is reviewed, someone will stop it. That creates a sense of confidence, a belief that the system is comprehensive. But detection is not absolute. It is conditional. It depends on thresholds, rules, and parameters, and those conditions define what becomes visible. Anything that falls within an acceptable range may never trigger attention, even if it is part of a larger fraud event.

This creates an illusion of coverage: activity appears monitored but isn't fully understood.

The Problem With Anomaly-Based Detection

Most detection systems rely on identifying what is different. Most of the time, they look at a transaction that is larger than usual. They also look at a login from an unfamiliar location. They also look for patterns that deviate from historical behavior. These are useful indicators, but they are not always present. Modern fraud often avoids extremes. It operates within limits, mirrors legitimate activity, and stays close enough to normal to avoid triggering alerts. That creates a blind spot: the system looks for what is unusual while fraud is designed to look usual.

Fragmentation Across Systems

Fraud rarely happens in a single step. It unfolds across multiple interactions. An email introduces the situation, but A call reinforces it, and a transaction completes it. Different systems may process each event and evaluate it independently. When evaluated independently, they often appear legitimate. The email looks normal. The call sounds reasonable. The transaction fits expected behavior. But when viewed together, they form a pattern, and that pattern reveals fraud.

The problem is that this pattern is not always visible in real time. Information is fragmented, distributed across systems, and separated by process. Without connection, you lose the full picture.

The Role of Timing

Timing is one of the most critical weaknesses in fraud detection. A delay often exists between when something happens and when it is reviewed. A transaction may appear normal in real time. Only later, when additional context becomes available, does it begin to look suspicious. By then, the outcome has already occurred, the funds have moved, access has been granted. Information has been exposed.

Fraud operates in real time. Detection often operates after the fact. And that gap creates opportunity.

The Normality Problem

One of the most difficult challenges in fraud detection is normality. When activity appears normal, it does not trigger concern. It doesn't demand attention or require deeper analysis. But normal activity can still be fraudulent. Some examples include:

- Payment that fits within expected ranges.
- A login that uses valid credentials.
- A request that aligns with routine behavior.

Each of these may appear safe, but without context, you can't fully understand them. Without understanding, you can't properly evaluate them.

A Real-World Breakdown

Consider a scenario involving business email compromise. An employee receives an email from a vendor. The request is to update payment instructions. The explanation is simple. The relationship is real. The request is processed. The payment is sent. From a detection standpoint, everything appears normal. No transaction amount is unusual, no access is unauthorized, and no anomaly is obvious. But when viewed in context, the situation changes. The email was fraudulent. Someone altered the account. The payment was misdirected.

The failure wasn't in the detection process. It was in the connection. The signals existed, but they were not connected in time.

Reframing Detection

Instead of asking: "Why wasn't this caught?" Ask: "What made this look normal?" Because fraud operates not in what is clearly wrong, but in what appears acceptable, this reframing shifts the focus from isolated events to patterns, from individual transactions to sequences, and from outcomes to progression.

The Limits of Traditional Detection

Traditional detection methods are effective at identifying clear anomalies. But they are less effective at identifying subtle patterns, especially when those patterns unfold over time, across different channels, and within normal behavior. This does not mean

detection systems are ineffective. It means they are incomplete. They address part of the problem, but not all of it.

Closing the Gap

Closing the gap in fraud detection requires a shift in perspective.

From: What happened to how it happened?

From: Single events to connected sequences.

From: Detection after the fact to recognition during the process. Because fraud is not just an event but a progression, understanding that progression allows it to be identified earlier.

Chapter 15

Fraudster's Playbook

Fraud is not random. It is not based on luck. And it is not as unpredictable as it often appears. Fraud is a process, one that is tested, refined, and repeated. Fraudsters do not guess; they learn and, more importantly, adapt. Understanding this is critical. Because fraud is not just about what is happening, it is about how it evolves.

Testing the System

Fraud often begins with small actions such as Low-risk activity and minimal exposure. The goal is not immediate gain; it is information. They accomplish this through A small transaction, a login attempt, or even a minor request.

Each action serves a purpose. They test the system. They reveal how controls respond. They provide insight into:

- What gets flagged?
- What gets approved?
- How quickly something is reviewed.

These early steps are not fraud itself. They are preparation. They help fraudsters understand the environment. Once they understand the environment, their approach changes.

Learning Through Outcomes

Every attempt provides feedback. A successful action confirms a method. A failed attempt provides information. Both outcomes are valuable. If a transaction is approved, it indicates that the parameters were acceptable. If it is declined, it reveals a boundary and tells them someone needs to adjust: someone can lower the amount, someone can change the timing, or someone can change the method.

This creates a feedback loop where each attempt improves the next. Over time, the approach becomes more effective. Not because it is more complex, but because it is more informed.

Operating Within Limits

Fraud does not always attempt to bypass controls. Often, it operates within them. Just below the level of detection within acceptable ranges, aligned with expected behavior. Examples can include:

- A transaction amount that does not trigger alerts.
- A login pattern that appears consistent.
- A request that fits within normal processes.

This is intentional because operating within limits reduces visibility. It avoids escalation. And it allows fraud to continue without interruption.

Scaling What Works

Once a method works, it is repeated across accounts, institutions, and channels. Fraud scales through repetition, not complexity. A process that works once can be applied again, with slight variations: different targets, different timing.

But the same underlying structure. This is how fraud grows, not through innovation alone, but through consistency.

Adapting to Controls

Every system has controls, rules, thresholds, and verification processes. Fraudsters do not ignore these. They study them. They observe how they function, and they adapt accordingly. If a system requires additional verification, they introduce urgency. If a threshold triggers alerts, they adjust amounts. If a pattern is flagged, they modify their behavior.

The goal is not to defeat the system directly; it is to work around it, to find the path of least resistance, and to follow it consistently.

The Advantage of Speed

One of fraud's key advantages is speed. Fraud can adapt quickly. Fraud can adapt quickly. Someone can adjust approaches immediately. Systems, on the other hand, often change more slowly. Rules must be updated. Someone must review the process and implement the controls. This creates a gap. Between how quickly fraud evolves and how quickly systems respond. Within that gap, fraud finds opportunity.

A Real-World Perspective

Consider a fraudster targeting account takeover. They begin with small attempts, testing login behavior, and observing how the system responds. They identify patterns, times when activity is less likely to be reviewed, and devices that appear less suspicious. They refine their approach. They introduce social engineering. They influence the user to provide credentials. They gain access. The process was not random. They develop, test, refine, and execute it.

Why This Matters

Understanding a fraudster's playbook changes perspective. Fraud is no longer seen as isolated events. It is seen as a process, a series of steps that build on each other, each one informed by previous outcomes. This explains why fraud can seem persistent, why similar patterns repeat, and why methods evolve: fraud is learning. And learning creates improvement.

The Role of Persistence

Fraud does not need to succeed every time; it only needs to succeed often enough. Failed attempts are not wasted. They provide information. They refine the approach. They improve the next attempt. This persistence creates an advantage. Because even unsuccessful actions contribute to future success. And over time, the process becomes more effective.

Breaking the Cycle

To disrupt fraud, you must understand this cycle. Not just what is happening, but how it develops.

- What is being tested?
- What is being learned?
- What patterns are being repeated?

These questions reveal insight. They expose the process behind the activity. Once you understand the process, it becomes easier to interrupt.

A Shift in Focus

Instead of focusing only on individual events, shift your attention to behavior over time. Because a single action does not define fraud; a series of actions does, each building on the last.

The Strategic Nature of Fraud

Fraud is not just opportunistic. It is often strategic, deliberate, and informed by experience. That makes it harder to detect using traditional methods alone. Traditional methods often focus on what is happening now. At the same time, fraud is shaped by what has already happened.

Looking Ahead

Fraudsters' playbook will keep evolving. New methods will emerge. They will use new tools. They will keep testing, learning, adapting, and repeating. And understanding that cycle is what allows it to be disrupted. Not after the fact, but during the process itself. Because once the process is recognized, the advantage begins to shift. From fraudsters to the system designed to stop them.

Chapter 16

Where Fraud Is Going Next

The Next Version Will Look Familiar

The next wave of fraud will not always arrive as a completely new kind of scam. More often, it will make familiar scams more convincing, faster, and harder to question in the moment. The message may still claim to be from a bank, a vendor, a relative, or a supervisor. The difference is that it may now sound more personal, look more polished, and arrive through several channels at once.

That matters because people do not make decisions based on a message alone. They react to context. A request that reflects a real relationship, mentions a recent purchase, or arrives from what appears to be a known number can feel credible before anyone has had time to examine it closely. The more believable the setting becomes, the more important it is to step outside the interaction and verify it independently.

Artificial Intelligence and Better Impersonation

Artificial intelligence gives fraudsters more ways to imitate legitimate communication. It can help produce cleaner messages, match a company or individual writing style, translate a request into natural language, and tailor the same scam to many different people. That does not mean every polished email or message is fraudulent. It does mean that poor grammar and obvious mistakes are becoming less reliable warning signs.

For that reason, the question is changing. Instead of asking whether a message looks professional, ask whether you verified the request through a channel the sender did not control. If payment instructions change, call a known number. If an account warning appears, open the official app or type the website yourself. If an executive request feels unusual, confirm it through an established internal process.

Voice and Video Will Require More Care

A familiar voice once felt like strong proof of identity. That is no longer always true. Short clips posted online, meeting recordings, and voicemail messages can give criminals material to imitate a person's voice. Someone can manipulate video as well. These tools do not need to be perfect to work. They only need to create enough confidence for someone to act before asking a second question.

The practical response is not to distrust everyone. It is to build a pause into sensitive requests. A transfer, a password reset, a request for gift cards, or a change to account details deserves a confirmation step, even when the voice, face, or message seems familiar. A prearranged callback number, a shared family phrase, or a separate approval process can turn a convincing impersonation into a stopped attempt.

Faster Payments Leave Less Room to Recover

Payment systems keep moving faster, which is convenient when everything is legitimate. It also means a bad decision can become a loss more quickly. Once money has been sent through an instant payment service, a wire, or another rapid method, there may be very little time to recover it. Fraudsters understand this. Their pressure often centers on the idea that there is no time to wait.

Treat that urgency as information, not a command. A real emergency may exist, but legitimate organizations can withstand a brief verification step. If a request cannot survive a pause, that is a reason to slow down, not speed up. Taking two minutes to call a known contact can protect far more than two minutes.

Personal Details Can Make a Scam Feel Real

More personal information is available online than most people realize. Public profiles, business websites, data breaches, and social media posts can reveal names, job titles, family connections, travel plans, and recent activity. Criminals can use those details to create a story that sounds specific enough to bypass ordinary skepticism.

Specificity is not proof. A message that knows your name, employer, or recent purchase may still be fraudulent. In fact, those details may be the hook. The safest response is to separate the information in the message from the decision it is asking you to make. A detail may be accurate, while the request itself is not.

The Best Defense Is a Deliberate Process

Technology will keep changing, but the strongest habits remain practical. Verify important requests outside the original message. Use contact information you already trust. Give employees and family members permission to pause when something feels rushed. Create clear approval steps for payments and account changes. These practices may feel simple, but they create the friction that fraud depends on people avoiding.

The goal is not to predict every new tool or every new story. It is to recognize when someone is trying to rush a decision. The hook may be more polished. The story may be more personal. The urgency may arrive through a voice call, a text, and an email at the same time. The final action, however, is still where the loss occurs, and that action can still be interrupted.

Looking Forward

Fraud will keep changing in appearance, but it will still rely on the same human pressures: trust, fear, urgency, and the desire to solve a problem quickly. Understanding that gives readers something more durable than a list of current scams. It gives them a way to think. When an interaction asks for immediate action, pause long enough to ask what it's requesting, why it must happen now, and how you can verify it independently. That pause is often where prevention begins.

Chapter 17

Real World Fraud Scenarios

Understanding fraud conceptually is important. Recognizing patterns, identifying stages, and analyzing behavior provide a strong foundation. But fraud is not experienced as a concept. It is experienced as a situation, a message,
a call, or a request that feels real in the moment. That is where understanding has to translate into recognition. This chapter brings fraud patterns into real-world context. Scenarios differ, and methods vary, but the underlying structure remains consistent: **Hook. Story. Urgency. Action.**

Once you recognize that structure in real situations, it becomes much easier to spot fraud as it unfolds.

Scenario 1: The "Safe Account" Transfer

A customer receives a phone call from someone claiming to be their bank. The caller explains that suspicious activity has occurred on the account and frames the situation as urgent. The caller tells the customer their funds are at risk and must be moved to a "safe account" for protection.

The explanation is clear, the tone is professional, and the request feels necessary.

The customer logs in, initiates a transfer, and sends the funds. From their perspective, they acted responsibly. They followed instructions and protected their accounts. In reality, a fraudster controlled the destination account.

Pattern: **Hook → A call from the bank Story → Account compromised. Urgency → Immediate protection required. Action → Transfer funds**

Scenario 2: Business Email Compromise

An employee receives an email that appears to come from a vendor. The message references a current invoice and says the payment details have changed. The explanation is simple, and the request feels routine. The employee updates the payment information and processes the payment.

Days later, the real vendor follows up. The invoice remains unpaid, and the funds were sent to a fraudulent account. Nothing about the request seemed unusual because it aligned with normal business activity.

Pattern: **Hook → Email from vendor Story → Updated payment instructions Urgency → Payment needs to be completed. Action → Send funds.**

Scenario 3: Check Fraud with Social Engineering

A customer is contacted with an opportunity and told they will receive payment for a job, service, or reimbursement. The explanation varies, but the structure remains consistent. A check arrives and appears legitimate, often for more than expected. The scammer instructs the customer to deposit it and send a portion back. Because the funds appear available, they follow the instructions and complete the transfer.

Days later, the check is returned, and the loss becomes real.

Pattern: **Hook → Opportunity introduced. Story → Payment explanation. Urgency → Funds must be returned quickly. Action → Send money.**

Scenario 4: Account Takeover

A customer receives a message indicating suspicious activity and is prompted to verify.

their account. The message looks legitimate, and the process feels familiar. They click the link, enter their credentials, and provide a verification code.

Moments later, a fraudster logs in, transfers funds, and takes control of the account.

Pattern: **Hook → Security alert Story → Account verification required. Urgency → Immediate action needed. Action → Provide credentials.**

Scenario 5: Internal Impersonation

An employee receives a message that appears to come from a senior executive. The message is direct, references a business matter, and requests a transfer.

The tone is urgent, and the employee acts quickly without questioning the request. The funds are sent. Later, they discover the message was fraudulent. The executive never made the request.

Pattern: **Hook → Message from executive • Story → Business-related request • Urgency → Immediate action required. Action → Transfer funds**

What These Scenarios Show

Each scenario is different in method, target, and outcome. But the structure remains the same. The interaction begins with attention, builds through context, accelerates with urgency, and concludes with action. This consistency is what makes fraud both effective and predictable. The details change. The pattern does not.

Why Recognition Matters

Fraud is hardest to detect at the final stage. By the time action occurs, the process is already complete in principle. The decision has been made, and the outcome is in

motion. Earlier in the sequence, however, there is still opportunity, at the hook, within the
story, and when urgency first appears. These are the moments where recognition matters most, because they are the points where the process can still be interrupted.

The Importance of Slowing Down

One of the most effective ways to disrupt fraud is to slow it down. Fraud depends on speed and progression, moving from one stage to the next without interruption. Slowing the process introduces friction. It creates space for questions, verification, and reconsideration.

Even a brief pause can make a meaningful difference. When the sequence is disrupted, the outcome can change.

Seeing the Pattern in Real Time

The goal is not to memorize specific scenarios. Fraud will keep evolving, and new methods will emerge. What remains constant is the pattern. The focus should not only be on what is happening, but on how it is unfolding.

Once the sequence becomes visible, the interaction becomes easier to interpret and challenge.

From Awareness to Action

Understanding fraud is not enough. It must be applied in real time. Recognition requires awareness, attention, and a willingness to pause, question, and verify. The difference between detection and prevention is timing, and timing depends on recognition.

The Final Insight

Fraud does not need to be complex to be effective. It only needs to be believable. Believability is built through structure:

- Hook
- Story
- Urgency

- Action

This structure appears in every scenario, every method, and every interaction. Once it is understood, it becomes easier to recognize, not just in examples, but in real situations.

That is where real value lies: not in understanding fraud after it happens, but in recognizing it while it is happening, when outcomes can still be changed, and prevention is still possible.

Conclusion

Understanding Fraud Differently

The goal is not just to recognize fraud after it happens. It is to identify it while it is happening, and to respond in a way that interrupts the process. The following takeaways provide a practical framework for doing exactly that.

Recognize the Sequence, Not Just the Event

Do not focus only on the final action. Look at how the situation developed.

Ask:

- How did this interaction begin?
- What context was provided?
- What led to this decision?

Fraud is not a single event. It is a sequence. And understanding that sequence is the first step in identifying it.

Question: What Feels Normal

Fraud often appears legitimate. That is intentional.

Instead of asking:

- "Does this look suspicious?" Ask:
- "Why does this look legitimate right now?"

This small shift creates awareness. And awareness creates the opportunity to pause and verify.

Slow Down the Process

Fraud depends on speed, movement, and uninterrupted progression. Slowing the process introduces friction. It creates time to think, verify, and question. Even a brief pause can disrupt the sequence. Verify Outside the Interaction: Don't rely solely on the information in the request. Use independent verification:

- A separate call
- A known contact
- A trusted source

Fraud often controls interaction. Verification within that interaction may not be reliable.

Pay Attention to Urgency

Urgency is one of the strongest indicators of fraud, not because it is always fraudulent, but because it changes how people make decisions. When something requires immediate action, ask:

- Why now?
- What happens if I wait? This helps separate real urgency from manufactured pressure.

Look Beyond the Transaction A transaction may appear normal. A login may seem valid. A request may feel routine. But context matters. Ask:

- What led to the action?
- What influenced the decision?

Understanding the context provides clarity that the action alone cannot.

Recognize Influence

Fraud is not just about deception. It is about influence, guiding decisions, shaping perception, and encouraging action

Recognizing when interaction is influencing behavior is critical because influence drives the outcome.

Focus on Early Intervention

The earlier you recognize fraud, the easier it is to stop, especially within the first three stages of the fraud pattern.

These are the stages where intervention is most effective. Waiting until the final step limits options.

Apply the Pattern Consistently

- **Hook. Story. Urgency. Action**

Use this pattern as a framework, not just for analysis, but for recognition. When an interaction begins, consider where it fits within the sequence. Once the pattern is visible, the interaction becomes clearer and easier to respond to.

Final Takeaway

Fraud is not just something that happens. It is something that unfolds. Once that process is understood, it becomes easier to see, not just after the fact, but in real time. Because the goal is not just to detect fraud, it is to prevent it. And prevention begins with recognition, at the moment when the outcome can still be changed.

About the Author

Christopher Biggar is the author of Fraud Aspect, a practical guide to recognizing the patterns that drive modern fraud. Visit christopherbiggar.com for additional resources and future books. In Fraud Aspect, he helps readers understand fraud as a behavioral pattern, not just a financial crime issue. His goal is to make it easier to recognize how fraud progresses and how a timely pause can prevent loss.

His writing centers on how fraud develops in real situations, how influence shapes decisions, and why many effective scams succeed because they appear legitimate.

Christopher brings a practical perspective to the gap between detection and reality. He is particularly interested in how fraud adapts to systems, processes, and human behavior, and how people and organizations can improve prevention by recognizing patterns earlier.

www.ingramcontent.com/pod-product-compliance
Lightning Source LLC
LaVergne TN
LVHW010737061126
851857LV00014B/1528